# Coming Home to You

All the good times and hard times — the laughter and tears. For the rest of my life, no matter where I go, or what I do — My Favorite Place On Earth....

I close my eyes and the memories of home rush to greet me.

will always be ....Home

D. Morgan © 1993

*D. Morgan*

HARVEST HOUSE PUBLISHERS
EUGENE, OREGON

# Coming Home to You

Text Copyright © 2000 Harvest House Publishers

Eugene, Oregon 97402

ISBN 0-7369-0202-3

Artwork designs are reproduced under license from © Arts Uniq'®, Inc., Cookeville, TN and may not be reproduced without permission. For information regarding art prints featured in this book, please contact:

Arts Uniq'
P.O. Box 3085
Cookeville, TN 38502
800-223-5020

Scriptures are from the Holy Bible, New International Version®. Copyright © 1973, 1978, 1984 by the International Bible Society. Used by permission of Zondervan Publishing House; and from the Living Bible, Copyright © 1971 owned by assignment by Illinois Regional Bank N.A. (as trustee). Used by permission of Tyndale House Publishers, Inc., Wheaton, Illinois 60189. All rights reserved.

Harvest House Publishers has made every effort to trace the ownership of all poems and quotes. In the event of a question arising from the use of a poem or quote, we regret any error made and will be pleased to make the necessary correction in future editions of this book.

Design and production by Koechel Peterson & Associates,
Minneapolis, Minnesota.

**Printed in the United States of America.**

00 01 02 03 04 05 06 07 08 09 / BG / 10 9 8 7 6 5 4 3 2 1

There's a little bit of heaven
'Round the corner,
Take a right.
A cozy little cottage
With a little kitchen light.
A refuge when I'm weary—
A comfort when I'm blue—
There's a little bit of heaven
Coming home to you...

D. MORGAN

Sweet is the hour that brings us home,

Where all will spring to meet us;

Where hands are striving, as we come,

To be the first to greet us.

ELIZA COOK

*He makes his home*
*where the living is best.*

LATIN PROVERB

I close my eyes and the memories of home rush to greet me. All the good times and hard times

D. Morgan © 1993

the laughter and tears. For the rest of my life,

My home is a treasure chest, in which I collect memories of my family and friends.

no matter where I go, or what I do —

My
Favorite
Place
On
Earth....

will always be

CLARA FERREE-SMITH

......Home

*Home*

For all your patience when I was difficult,
For being there everytime I needed help
For all your understanding when I was impossible,
But most of all
For your unconditional love for me

Mom and Dad

All My Heart

D. Morgan © 1990.

*I will always love you*
*With all my heart.*

'Tis joy to him that toils, when toil is o'er,

To find a home waiting, full of happy things.

EURIPEDES

*Go home in peace.*

THE BOOK OF 1 SAMUEL

Mother was a born singer. The first sound in the morning was her voice as she went about the house singing like a lark, and the last sound at night was the same cheery sound, for the girls never grew too old for that familiar lullaby.

LOUISA MAY ALCOTT
LITTLE WOMEN

*All that I am or hope to be,*
*I owe to my mother.*

ABRAHAM LINCOLN

*Once upon*

*My feelings With*

*I know I'm home by the fragrance of my mother's*

SUSAN WALES

a yesterday ~

You kissed my little hurts away.

My source of comfort, strength and pride ~

You were always by my side.

or you are like no other ~

ll my heart......

......I Love You Mother

© 1989 D. Morgan

kitchen.

Mother

Of all good times remembered
When I was very young,

My heart holds most dear.....

...The time My Daddy spent with me.

Daddy

©1989 D. Morgan

*Some may own castles on the banks of the Rhine,*
*and hire an orchestra each evening at nine;*
*But richer than I they will never be . . .*
*I had a Dad who spent time with me.*

D. MORGAN

Mama took me on her lap and com—
forted me; and when I had quieted, Papa
held me in his arms as he did when I was
a baby. I can still feel the sensation of
safety as I put my head upon his shoulder.

CORRIE TEN BOOM
*IN MY FATHER'S HOUSE*

*David returned home to*
*bless his family.*

THE BOOK OF 1 CHRONICLES

The door of the little house opened, and a

warm glow of firelight flickered out into the

dusk. Gilbert lifted Anne from the buggy

and led her into the garden, through the little

gate between the ruddy-tipped firs, up the

trim, red path to the sandstone step.

"Welcome home," he whispered, and hand

in hand they stepped over the threshold of

their house of dreams.

L.M. MONTGOMERY
ANNE OF GREEN GABLES

If I could do it all over again ~ and start my
..... Many a thing I'd do differently

*If a man has recently married...for one year he is to be free to stay at home and bring happiness to the wife he has married.*

THE BOOK OF DEUTERONOMY

But I'd do it again — with — you.

D. Morgan © 1993

The more one does and sees and feels,

the more one is able to do, and the more

genuine may be one's appreciation of

fundamental things like home, and love,

and understanding companionship.

AMELIA EARHART

"Home" is any four walls that
enclose the right person.

HELEN ROWLAND

*Memories in*

*Let the wife make the husband glad to come home.*

*And the husband make the wife sorry to see him leave.*

MARTIN LUTHER

*There is room in the smallest cottage for a happy loving pair.*

JOHANN FRIEDRICH VON SCHILLER

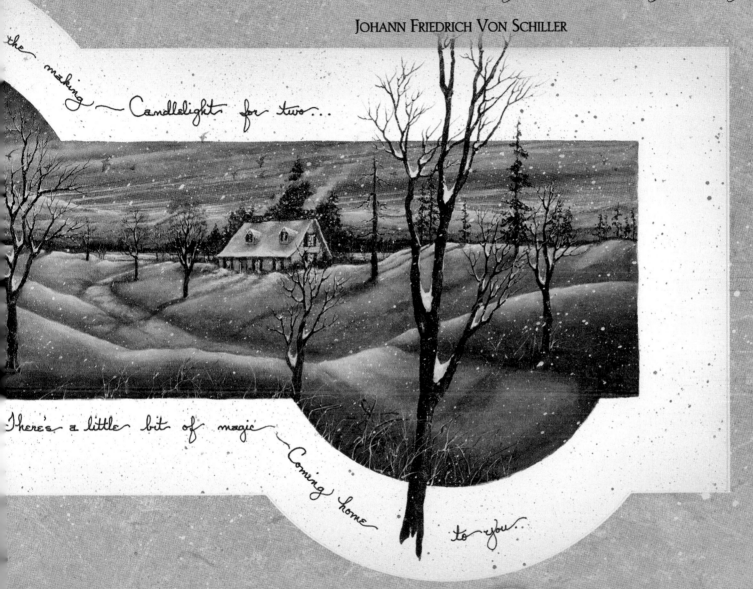

the making ~ Candlelight for two...

There's a little bit of magic ~ Coming home to you...

Loving Pair

There is no happiness comparable to that of the first handclasp, when one asks, "Do you love me?" and the other replies, "Yes."

GUY DE MAUPASSAIT

Let nothing break the sweet ties that now bind you together, and do not be as strangers to each other when you should be closest friends.

LOUISA MAY ALCOTT

Husband Dear

You're a great little wife, and I don't

know what I would do without you."

And as he spoke he put his arms about

her and kissed her, and she forgot all care

at that moment. And, forgetting it all, she

sang as she washed the dishes, and sang

as she made the beds, and the song was

heard next door, and a woman there

caught the refrain and sang also, and two

homes were happier because he had told

her that sweet old story—the story of the

love of a husband for a wife.

AUTHOR UNKNOWN

My morning sun ~ My evening star ~ More than I ever dreamed you'd be ~ My husband dear ~ You are. You are all things in life to me.

D. Morgan © 1995

*It* takes a hundred men to make an

encampment, but it takes only the influence

of one woman to make a home. I not only

admire woman as the most beautiful object

ever created, but I reverence her as the

redeemed glory of humanity, the sanctuary of

all perfect qualities of heart and head...The

one thing in this world that is considered

constant, the only peak that rises above the

clouds, the window in which the light burns

forever, the one star that darkness cannot

quench, is woman's love. It rises to the low-

est depths, it forgives the most cruel injuries.

A woman's love is the perfume of the heart.

ROBERT INGERSOLL

*Among Are Simple Cozy*

*Old love      letters tied with*

The dearest things I know
where the wild flowers grow —
pleasures ~ gentle faces
little wayside places . . . . .

D. Morgan © 1990

blue —— the way I feel when I'm with you.

*Dearest Things*

A splendid team, my wife and I;

She washes dishes, and I dry.

I sometimes pass her back a dish

To give another cleansing swish.

She sometimes holds up to the light

A glass I haven't dried just right

But mostly there is no complaint,

Or it is courteous and faint,

For I would never care to see

The washing job consigned to me,

And though the things I dry still drip,

She keeps me for companionship.

RICHARD ARMOUR

# Companionship

The test of pleasure is

the memory that it

leaves behind.

JEAN PAUL RICHTER

together

Would surely be too few

with you

D. Morgan © 1996

My dear sister.
The best memories always surface remembering our childhood. And with each passing year I realize more and more how very blessed I am that you are my sister. I love you.

For there is no friend like a sister

In calm or stormy weather;

To cheer one on the tedious way,

To fetch one if one goes astray,

To lift one if one totters down,

To strengthen whilst one stands.

CHRISTINA ROSSETTI

*Sisters make the real conversations…not the saying but the never needing to say is what counts.*

MARGARET LEE RUNBECK

*A sister can be seen*
*as someone who is both*
*ourselves and very*
*much not ourselves—a*
*special kind of double.*

Toni Morrison

Once,
Someone Held My Hand...
And wiped away a tear ~
That Someone very Special...
Was you... my Sister dear

D. Morgan © 1989

Sister Dear

Till Little Arliss got us mixed up in that bear

fight, I guess I'd been looking on him about like

most boys look on their little brothers. I liked

him, all right, but I didn't have a lot of use for

him...But that day when I saw him in the spring,

so helpless against that angry she bear, I learned

different. I knew then that I loved him as much

as I did Mama and Papa, maybe in some ways

even a little bit more.

FRED GIPSON
OLD YELLER

*the years Of bandages*

*Dear Brother, after all*

*Dearest friend*

*D. Morgan © 1989*

knees
and
Broken
Hearts,

You
Are
My...

*A brother is a friend provided by nature.*

Legouve Pere

*He has also brotherly pride, which with some brotherly*

*affection, makes him a very kind and careful guardian*

*of his sister; and you will hear him generally cried up as*

*the most attentive and best of brothers.*

Jane Austen
Pride and Prejudice

Dear Brother

Our home joys are the most delightful earth

affords, and the joy of parents in their children is,

the most holy joy of humanity. It makes their

hearts pure and good, it lifts men up to their

Father in heaven.

JOHANN HEINRICH PESTALOZZI

*Where thou art, that is home.*

EMILY DICKINSON

*and when*

*Home*

Let us guide our children with wisdom ~
Let us listen to their problems
And help them find solutions.
Let us give them
Unconditional
Love ~

No

Matter

What . . . . . .

they are grown,
        let us find the courage to let go.                    D. Morgan © 1990

R. Morgan © 1987

*I* don't think I have any words in which to tell the meeting of the mother and daughters. Such hours are beautiful to live, but very hard to describe, so I will leave it to the imagination of my readers, merely saying that the house was full of genuine happiness...

LOUISA MAY ALCOTT
LITTLE WOMEN

*I've pressed the ribbon from her hair...*
*And saved his favorite shirt to wear.*

D. MORGAN

My Dear Mary,

How lonely the house seems—I never knew before how well you helped to fill it... Ever since you went away, I have been wondering if it was as hard for you to go out into the world as it was for me to have you go... If there is anything in my life that can be of value to you, I want you to have it; if I can save you a stumble or a single false step, I want to do it, but the only way I can do it is to know your heart.

Your loving mother...

Florence Wenderoth Saunders

"LETTERS TO A BUSINESS GIRL"

I remember when you were My Little Girl...as much a part of me as my right arm. My every breath and step held you in mind. Then suddenly, one morning—you were gone. I was not finished with you—but we must love our children enought to let them go— but in my heart . . . you will always be . . . My Little Girl

My Little Girl

D. MORGAN

Boys are found everywhere—on top of, underneath,

inside of, climbing on, swinging from, running

around or jumping to...A boy is Truth with dirt on

its face, Beauty with a cut on its finger, Wisdom with

bubble gum in its hair, and the Hope of the future

with a frog in its pocket.

ALAN BECK

Tattered little teddy bear looks so lonesome on the stair,

Rocky horse still standing tall waits for you just down the hall.

All the other playthings rest within the toy treasure chest.

Little childhood play is done. You've become a man, my son.

Yet in the long ago and far away, there still lives....

....That Precious Little Boy At Play.

Children are a gift from the Lord.

THE BOOK OF PSALMS

A Little Child

*I do not love him*
*because he is good,*
*But because he is*
*my little child.*

AUTHOR UNKNOWN

*'Tis a happy thing to be the*

*father of many sons.*

WILLIAM SHAKESPEARE

A. Morgan © 1997

## A LITTLE FACE

A little face to look at,
A little face to kiss;
Is there anything, I wonder,
That's half so sweet as this?

A little cheek to dimple
When smiles begin to grow,
A little mouth betraying
Which way the kisses go.

A slender little ringlet,
A rosy little ear,
A little chin to quiver
When falls the little tear.

A little hand so fragile,
All through the night to hold;
Two little feet so tender,
To tuck in from the cold.

Two eyes that watch the sunbeam
That with the shadow plays;
A darling little baby,
To kiss and love always.

FROM *BEAUTIFUL GEMS OF SENTIMENT*

D. Morgan© 1994

"So, if I've got on at all, you may thank these two for it." And he laid one hand gently on his grandfather's head, and the other on Amy's golden one, for the three were never far apart.

LOUISA MAY ALCOTT
LITTLE WOMEN

I smiled at Grandpa.
Grandpa's my best friend.

PATRICIA HERMES
A PLACE FOR JEREMY

Heidi had rushed up to him...
him again to say more than

His Grandpa

Who thinks that we are too severe?
His Grandpa.
Who thinks the modern doctors queer?
His Grandpa.
Who takes him walking down the street,
And shows him off to all they meet,
And buys him stuff he shouldn't eat?
His Grandpa.
Who will not let the youngster cry?
His Grandpa.
Who slips him candy on the sly?
His Grandpa.
Who scoffs at every law we make
To save him from the tummy ache,
And fills him full of chocolate cake?
His Grandpa.

I remember all

The

The

The ice cream

No one in the

and flung her arms around his neck, unable in the excitement of seeing

"Grandfather! grandfather! grandfather!" over and over again.

JOHANNA SPYRI *HEIDI*

the good times we've had together ...

funny little songs ~

piggy back rides

cones. — How you always listened
To my problems.
world could ever be as special as......
My
Grandaddy.

D. Morgan © 1989

Who thinks that we are silly fools?

His Grandpa.

Who mocks all hygienic rules?

His Grandpa.

Who laughs at all his willful ways
And thinks him cute when he displays

His temper to the public gaze?

His Grandpa.


And yet who was it once was stern?

His Grandpa.

Who made his son obedience learn?

His Grandpa.

Who was it once pronounced the word,

Which now he says is most absurd,

That children should be seen, not heard?

His Grandpa.

EDGAR GUEST

*"I do think that families are the most beautiful things in all the world!" burst out Jo.*

LOUISA MAY ALCOTT
*LITTLE WOMEN*

No matter where I travel

There's just no other place

*Or just how far I roam*

*Quite as nice as Home.*

## My Family

Funny little wriggly toes
With a button for a nose,
Hardly fits at all in clothes,
That's brother!

Sweet and smiling all the day
Fine at kissing hurts away;
Says that being mean won't pay
That's mother!

Big and loud and lots of fun.
Calls me "Kid," calls Mother "Hon."
When I'm bad? Well, gee, I run.
That's father!

Smarty! Thinks she knows it all.
Dresses like a baby doll.
Kissed her fella in the hall.
That's sister!

Then there's me. Well, I ain't much
Got a dog, his name is Dutch.
Fine at chasing cats and such.
That's me!

*Family*

May A. Feehan

Kitchens are made for long talks and close friends, loving families and lots of laughter. Kitchens are made for daydreams and growing things.

Quiet times and reflective moments, for sharing and preparing the blessings of life.

AUTHOR UNKNOWN

standing,

difficult,
were kind.

I needed a friend,
You were there for me
special

If you come cheerily,

Here shall be jest for you;

If you come wearily,

Here shall be rest for you.

If you come borrowing,

Gladly we'll loan to you;

If you come sorrowing,

Love shall be shown to you.

Under our thatch, friend,

Place shall abide for you,

Touch but the latch, friend,

The door will swing wide for you!

NANCY BYRD TURNE

D. Morgan © 1990

—a more wonderful step-parent than you.

*Where can a person be better than in the bosom of their family?*

MARMONTEL GRETRY

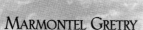

*We* are all here,
Father, mother,
Sister, brother,
All who hold each other dear.
Each chair is filled; we're all at home!
Tonight let now cold stranger come.
It is not often thus around
Our old familiar hearth we're found.
Bless, then, the meeting and the spot;
For once be every care forgot;
Let gentle Peace assert her power,
And kind Affection rule the hour.
We're all—all here.

CHARLES SPRAGUE

*We* spoke of gypsies,
World affairs,
Of fiction, fact, and fable—

Of Poe and Frost,
Paradise Lost,
No other Rhett but Gable.

We shared our failures,
Hopes and dreams...

Around
the
kitchen
table.

D. MORGAN

*Favorite Things*

*In our home, come share with us a time of love and laughter.*

*Favorite with dearest friends...make memories everafter.*

D. Morgan

This family is achieving something!

Within this home are gaiety, laughter,

cooperation, understanding, neighborliness,

community mindedness, and world

concern...as you enter you are conscious

not of architecture or an interior decorator's

area. This home has...atmosphere.

It is a mingling of hospitality,

refinement, and good cheer.

RUTH MCA BROWN

*Nor need we power or splendor, wide*

*good, the true, the tender—these*

SARAH J. HALE

hall or lordly dome; the

form the wealth of home.

No place on earth I'ee ever find —

...... Like home — so gentle on my mind.

D. Morgan © 1987

*I have been very happy with my*

*homes, but homes really are no more*

*than the people who live in them.*

NANCY REAGAN

Aunt Em had just come out of the house

to water the cabbages when she looked up

and saw Dorothy running toward her.

"My darling child!" she cried, folding the little

girl in her arms and covering her face

with kisses, "where in the world did you

come from?"

"From the Land of Oz," said Dorothy gravely.

"And here is Toto, too. And oh, Aunt Em!

I'm so glad to be at home again!"

L. FRANK BAUM
THE WIZARD OF OZ

I'll keep a candle in the window
The home fires always burn
There's a prayer on my lips
Until your safe return.

Let no one ever come to you without

expression of God's kindness:

D. Morgan ©1991

*leaving better and happier. Be the living kindness in your face, kindness in your eyes, kindness in your smile.*

MOTHER TERESA

*Home Again*

Winter
Longs to
Linger
In the
Chill
Of
Afternoon

Winter is the time for comfort, for good food and warmth, for the touch of a friendly hand and for a talk beside the fire: it is the time for home.

DAME EDITH SITWELL

Cheerfully share your home...

THE BOOK OF 1 PETER

Time for Home

*You always know that
you are home when a house
speaks to you—and they do
speak, the best of them.*

MARIANNE GINGHER

*Hollyhocks
and
Butterflies...
Sing
"A
Summer
Song."*

D. Morgan © 1998

*Having a place to go—is a home.*

*Having someone to love—is a family.*

*Having both—is a blessing.*

DONNA HEDGES

May this home be full of love, with His richest blessings from above. From morning sun to evening prayer — we count on Him....

....He's Always There.

D. Morgan © 1994